CELEBRATING THE NAME EMMA

Celebrating the Name Emma

Walter the Educator

Silent King Books

Copyright © 2024 by Walter the Educator

All rights reserved. No part of this book may be reproduced in any manner whatsoever without written permission except in the case of brief quotations embodied in critical articles and reviews.

First Printing, 2024

Disclaimer
This book is a literary work; poems are not about specific persons, locations, situations, and/or circumstances unless mentioned in a historical context. This book is for entertainment and informational purposes only. The author and publisher offer this information without warranties expressed or implied. No matter the grounds, neither the author nor the publisher will be accountable for any losses, injuries, or other damages caused by the reader's use of this book. The use of this book acknowledges an understanding and acceptance of this disclaimer.

dedicated to everyone with the first name of Emma

EMMA

Echoes dance with glee,

EMMA

Resides a name, a symphony:

EMMA

Emma, fair and tenderly,

EMMA

In whispers soft, a melody.

EMMA

From dawn's embrace to twilight's glow,

EMMA

Her name in hearts, a river's flow,

EMMA

.

With each syllable, a radiant show,

EMMA

A beacon bright, aglow.

EMMA

In fields of dreams where wildflowers bloom,

EMMA

Emma's name, a sweet perfume,

EMMA

A gentle breeze, a sacred loom,

EMMA

Weaving tales in every room.

EMMA

In realms of ink where poets dwell,

EMMA

Emma's name, a mystic spell,

EMMA

A quill's embrace, a secret well,

EMMA

Unveiling stories, time will tell.

EMMA

In whispers hushed and secrets shared,

EMMA

Emma's name, a treasure rare,

EMMA

A promise kept, a soul laid bare,

EMMA

In love's embrace, beyond compare.

EMMA

In halls of memory, where shadows play,

EMMA

Emma's name, a light of day,

EMMA

A whispered prayer, a pathway,

EMMA

Guiding souls along the way.

EMMA

In laughter's echo, tears that fall,

EMMA

Emma's name, a hearth for all,

EMMA

A gentle touch, a whispered call,

EMMA

In every heart, a sacred hall.

EMMA

In realms unseen, beyond the veil,

EMMA

Emma's name, a timeless tale,

A constellation, a celestial trail,

EMMA

In every whisper, we prevail.

EMMA

So raise your voice, let it be known,

EMMA

Emma's name, a cornerstone,

EMMA

In every heart, a precious stone,

EMMA

In every soul, a throne.

EMMA

For in the tapestry of life, we see,

EMMA

Emma's name, a symphony,

EMMA

A timeless song, eternally,

EMMA

In every heart, forever free.

EMMA

ABOUT THE CREATOR

Walter the Educator is one of the pseudonyms for Walter Anderson. Formally educated in Chemistry, Business, and Education, he is an educator, an author, a diverse entrepreneur, and he is the son of a disabled war veteran. "Walter the Educator" shares his time between educating and creating. He holds interests and owns several creative projects that entertain, enlighten, enhance, and educate, hoping to inspire and motivate you.

Follow, find new works, and stay up to date
with Walter the Educator™
at WaltertheEducator.com

www.ingramcontent.com/pod-product-compliance
Lightning Source LLC
LaVergne TN
LVHW052009060526
838201LV00059B/3938